Introduction

Responding to Literature 1–3 is a collection of classroom-tested teaching strategies and student activities that promote rereading and generate literature response in numerous formats. This resource is comprised of meaningful and motivating activities that are easily adaptable to any literature selection.

Before young students can read into, through, and beyond a story to think, talk, and write critically about it, they must first learn to recognize and recall key story events and details. After students have processed this information, they can begin to classify, make inferences, and analyze a story on a personal level of understanding.

Research has confirmed that the more students read, the better they read; and the more they read familiar text, the more automatically they recognize words. The more automatically students recognize words, the more fluently they read. The more fluent students become, the more expressive and confident they are in their reading. And so goes the reading cycle for successful readers!

The exciting rereading strategies and literature response activities in *Responding to Literature 1–3* make it easy for your students to reread text and interact with any book selection. This book includes

- ready-to-use reproducibles
- step-by-step directions for working with your students on various literature selections
- rationale for developing the skills presented
- ideas for extending each activity

This resource provides students with the opportunity to embark on the journey of reading and the pleasure that comes along with it.

Getting Started

Responding to Literature 1–3 contains numerous activities, in various motivational formats, to stimulate students' understanding of key vocabulary and basic story elements.

Building Fluent Readers

Students become fluent readers when their word recognition increases, they understand print concepts, and they read orally with expression. This resource provides the strategies and activities needed to increase fluency while developing confident readers who enjoy reading.

Strengthening Comprehension

As fluency increases, comprehension strengthens. This resource is filled with dozens of activities that help students strengthen comprehension by focusing on key elements such as accessing prior knowledge, categorization, characterization, identifying the main character, predicting, retelling, and sequencing.

Using This Book

This book is divided into two sections. The activities in both sections are flexible and can be used to reinforce different skills throughout the year. Choose the lessons that work best with your students.

The Rereading Strategies section (see pages 5–11) presents fun, stimulating ways to encourage rereading. Vary the use of these strategies to have students reread any type of literature throughout the day in a variety of ways (e.g., shared reading, choral reading, guided reading, buddy reading, independent reading).

The Literature Response Activities section (see pages 12–63) includes a variety of teaching strategies and time-saving reproducibles. First, decide how you would like students to read the selection (e.g., independent reading, shared reading, or guided reading). Then, choose an activity, and copy a class set of the corresponding reproducible.

To ensure student success, it is important to model for students how to complete the activities in this resource before having students work independently. For example, photocopy an activity reproducible and enlarge it to chart size, or create a transparency of the reproducible. In a whole-group setting, lead the class step-by-step through the process indicated in the directions, always modeling your thinking about the process using the "think-aloud" procedure so students are cognizant of your every thought and action regarding the process from reading the story, to thinking about the story, to actually recording your response on the reproducible.

RESPONDING to LITERATURE 1–3
Activities That Build Confident Readers and Writers

Written by
Dr. Margaret Allen, Ph.D.

Editor: Sheri Samoiloff
Illustrator: Jenny Campbell
Cover Illustrator: Karl Edwards
Designer: Moonhee Pak
Cover Designer: Moonhee Pak
Art Director: Tom Cochrane
Project Director: Carolea Williams

Table of Contents

Add Some Sound

Purpose

To extend the meaning of the story by creating appropriate sound effects to add to the dramatic choral reading of the story

Procedure

Select a story with a variety of characters or objects for which students could create sound effects (e.g., animals, toys, machines). Brainstorm with students the sounds each character, toy, or machine makes. Decide together on the sound effects students will make during a read-aloud. Read aloud the story, and have the class make the sound effects, or have selected students make the sound effects at the appropriate time.

Be the One

Purpose

To emphasize reading with expression and to interpret all of the characters in the story by creating a different voice for each character

Procedure

After reading a story with speaking parts for multiple characters, discuss the characters with the class. Have students describe each character. Explain to students that by using a different voice for each character, they can interpret each character's personality as they read. Decide together on the "voice" for each character. Model the voice for each character. Have students reread the whole story using all of the character voices and a "normal" voice for narration.

Clapping Strategies

Purpose

To internalize the structure of rhythmic, rhyming text by feeling a steady beat during the reading

Procedure

Choose a story, poem, or chant that can be read with a rhythm. Demonstrate an age-appropriate clapping rhythm for students. For example, have students place their hands on their knees and then clap for the "Hands-Knees Clap," or have them clap, cross their right hand over to touch their left shoulder, clap again, and then cross their left hand over to touch their right shoulder for the "Cross-Shoulder Clap." Read the story, poem, or chant one sentence or line at a time, and invite students to repeat the words and practice their clapping rhythm to the words. Have students practice the rhythm several times until they can perform it fluidly. Have students use the same strategy with a song, such as "This Old Man" or "A-Hunting We Will Go." Write the words on a piece of chart paper, and teach the song to the class. Have students reread the song using the rhythmic clapping strategy.

Echo Chant Reading

Purpose

To hear and echo fluent reading of text

Procedure

Expressively read a page of text from a book, a song, or a poem one sentence at a time. Have students mimic your expression. Continue this process with the rest of the book, song, or poem.

Monster Reading

Purpose
To use a character voice during guided reading

Procedure
Select any short text with a monster theme. Read the story to the class. Ask students to think how a monster would sound. Invite them to imitate many different kinds of monsters. Then, have students use a selected monster voice and reread a page or the entire story.

Opera Reading

Purpose
To emphasize reading with expression and to have fun interpreting a story character's feelings

Procedure
Play a short opera selection for students, and describe how performers in an opera sing their characters' parts. Read aloud a story with numerous character parts. Then, select one character, and every time that character speaks have students sing the character's part to dramatize the feeling the character conveys.

Pairs Chairs Reading

Purpose

To read fluently with a partner during independent reading time; to listen while a partner reads and follow along until it is time to read

Procedure

Select a book with two main character parts, such as *City Mouse and Country Mouse* by Rozanne Lanczak Williams (Creative Teaching Press), *Yo! Yes!* by Chris Raschka (Orchard Books), or *The Chick and the Duckling* by Mirra Ginsburg (Econo-Clad Books). Read the book to the class. Divide the class into pairs. Have each pair of students place their chair backs in opposite directions (as shown). Give each pair a copy of the book. While one student reads a page, have the other student follow along and then read the next page. Have students read the entire book this way.

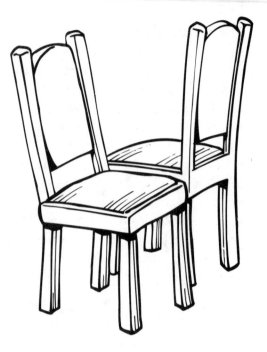

Read to the Beat

Purpose

To build oral reading fluency and reading enjoyment by internalizing the rhyme of the story

Procedure

Obtain a mini-keyboard. Before trying it with students, experiment with some of the keyboard's preprogrammed rhythms. Select a familiar rhythmic, rhyming text. Set the keyboard to play a programmed beat, and hold up a book for the class to read from. Prerecorded keyboard music or music with a strong beat will also work well for this strategy.

Robot Reading

Purpose

To help students who tend to read without pauses to read more fluently and naturally

Procedure

Write a short story, nursery rhyme, or poem on chart paper, and display it. Ask students to stand straight and move like a robot. Then, ask them to read the text "robot style" by using a robot-like voice and by taking a breath between each word in each sentence. Also, use this technique to help students understand that although it is fun to read like a robot once in a while to punctuate each word in the text, it is not fun to hear whole stories read robot style! Explain that "robot reading" is not fluent reading.

Select a Word

Purpose

To create awareness of high-frequency words and to increase automaticity with reading them

Procedure

Draw a large 4 x 5 square grid on the chalkboard. Write a high-frequency or vocabulary word in each square. Have a volunteer select a word and read it aloud. Invite the class to repeat the word. Cover the word with a sticky note. Continue the activity until all the words have been read. To extend the activity, erase a word after it has been read, and write a new word in the square.

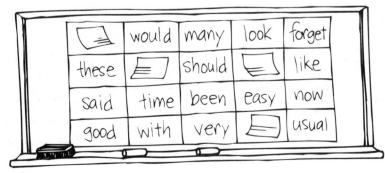

Sing It to Learn It

Purpose

To build oral reading fluency by learning to "chunk" the text into manageable portions through song

Procedure

Write the words to a poem or song on a piece of chart paper. Have students read the words chorally (together). Introduce the melody. Have students follow along as you sing the text. Then, have students sing the text.

Sound Punctuation

Purpose

To create awareness of the purpose of punctuation in a story; to help students who tend to read without pauses to read more fluently and naturally

Procedure

Select a page of text from any book with numerous punctuation marks. Demonstrate for students how to say *Pop* for a period, say *Shhh* for a comma, say *Hmmm* (voice going down) for a question mark, and *Hmmm* (voice going up) for an exclamation point. Demonstrate how to use these sounds while reading a page of text. Invite students to reread the text aloud and use the sounds to accentuate punctuation.

Stomp It

Purpose

To help young students understand "concept of print" by recognizing each word in the text

Procedure

Read a line of text with the class. Have students stand and, with alternating feet, stomp on each word to reread the text. This is a useful technique for students who tend to skim as they read or who try to read too quickly and skip words. This strategy is also useful when students need to expend extra energy before they can attend to their reading assignment!

STOMP

Whisper Reading

Purpose

To help students who often do not attend to their reading but merely mimic or "parrot" other students to concentrate on their own reading

Procedure

Read a line of text from a book using a well-modulated reading voice. Have students read the next line of text using a soft, "whisper" voice. Continue to alternate reading the book line by line with the class. Have students summarize what they read.

Character Comparisons

Purpose

This activity is designed to have students think critically about characters in the story and words to describe the characters.

Directions

1 Copy a class set of the Character Comparisons reproducible.

2 Choose a book to read to the class or for students to read independently.

3 After reading the story, have students discuss the characters.

4 Give each student a reproducible. Ask students to select one character from the story and draw a picture of the character in the center of the box.

5 Have students think of one word to describe the character, such as *big, mean, sweet, tall, bossy, happy,* or *smart,* and then write the word in the first blank of lines one, two, and three.

6 Have students write three other things that fit the one-word description in the second blank of lines one, two, and three. Have them draw pictures of these things in three corners of the box.

7 Invite students to write the character's name in the last blank.

Scary

Extension

Use this activity with a nonfiction book to have students create comparisons that describe animals, plants, rocks, or planets.

Name _____   Date _____

Character Comparisons

Choose a character from the story to draw in the center of the box. Think of one word to describe the character, and write it in the first blank of lines one, two, and three. Write three other things that fit the one-word description in the second blank of lines one, two, and three. Draw pictures of these things in three corners of the box. Write the character's name in the last blank.

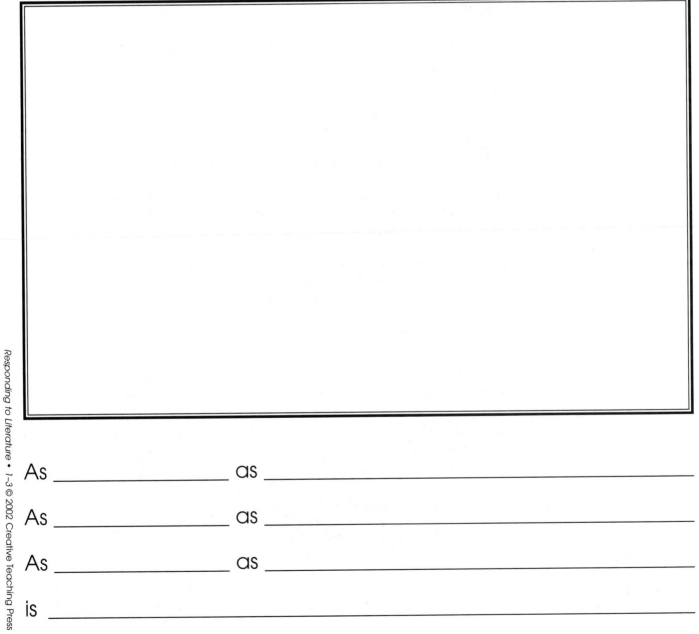

As _____ as _____

As _____ as _____

As _____ as _____

is _____

Choose a Mystery Character

Purpose

This activity is designed to help students recall details about characters and stories and use them to create a "mystery" for other students to solve.

Directions

1 Copy a class set of the Mystery Character Lift-a-Flap reproducible. Cut a 3½" x 6" (9 cm x 15 cm) construction paper strip for each student.

2 Choose numerous familiar books to read to the class or for students to read independently.

3 After reading the books, brainstorm with the class the characters, setting, and important details that occurred in each of the stories. Record student responses on the chalkboard or a piece of chart paper.

4 Ask each student to select a character from one of the stories but not reveal the name to anyone else.

5 Explain to the class that their character's identity is a secret and they will pretend to be detectives trying to identify each classmate's "mystery" character.

6 Give each student a reproducible and a construction paper strip.

7 Have students draw their mystery character in the box on the reproducible.

8 Ask them to glue the top part of their paper strip onto their reproducible to make a flap over their drawing.

9 Have students write three clues about their character in the form of a riddle. Have students begin each clue with the word "I." Clues may include what story the character is in, the character's personality traits, or how the character acted in the story. Invite students to orally present their clues, and have the class guess who the mystery character is.

Extension

Tape the flap closed on each completed reproducible. Number the reproducibles, and post them around the room. Have each student number a piece of writing paper. Invite students to take a Character Mystery Walk. Have them read each set of clues and then write a character's name next to the corresponding number on their paper. Remove the flaps, and invite students to check their answers.

Mystery Character Lift-a-Flap

Draw a picture of your character in the box. Glue the top of a construction paper strip to the top of the box. Write three clues about your character. Start each clue with the word "I."

```
+------------------------------------------------+
|                Glue Flap Here                  |
| - - - - - - - - - - - - - - - - - - - - - - -  |
|                                                |
|                                                |
|                                                |
|                                                |
|                                                |
|                                                |
|                                                |
+------------------------------------------------+
```

Clues

1. I _____

   _____

2. I _____

   _____

3. I _____

   _____

Who am I?

Responding to Literature • 1-3 © 2002 Creative Teaching Press

Dear Story Character

Purpose

This activity is designed to increase students' letter-writing ability in response to thought-provoking text. Students write to the character to suggest an alternative solution to the story problem, give the character advice on future actions, or compliment or chastise the character for his or her behavior.

Directions

 Copy a class set of the Character Letter reproducible.

 Choose a story to read to the class or for students to read independently.

❸ After reading the story, brainstorm with the class the part(s) of the story that seemed more important than the rest of the story, and discuss the character(s) in that part. Have students think about elements of the story such as a character's behavior, the story problem, or the solution. Record student responses on the chalkboard or a piece of chart paper.

❹ Give each student a reproducible. Have students express their thoughts about the character or the story in a letter to the character.

❺ Invite students to read their letter to a classmate.

Extension

Have students address an envelope to their character. Invite them to exchange letters and envelopes with another class that has also completed this assignment, or invite them to exchange letters with a classmate. Have the classmate write a reply in character.

Character Letter

Date _____

Dear _____,

I really like your story, _____.

I chose to write to you because _____

_____

_____.

I like the part of the story when _____

_____

_____

_____.

Your friendly reader,

_____

World's Greatest!!

Favorite Character Election

Purpose

This activity is designed to help students bring personal meaning to the story by selecting their favorite character.

Directions

 1 Copy a class set of the Favorite Character Election Ballot reproducible. Create a ballot box from a shoe box or cardboard box.

2 Choose a book to read to the class or for students to read independently.

3 After reading the story, have students discuss the characters in the story.

4 Give each student a reproducible. Ask students to select their favorite character from the story and write the character's name on the second line of the reproducible.

5 Have them draw a picture of their character in the frame.

6 Tell students to drop their completed ballot into the ballot box.

7 Invite the class to predict which character will get the most votes and explain why.

8 Count the votes together, and have the class determine who the winner is. Discuss with the class whether or not they felt the character deserved to win and why.

Extension

Turn the ballots into a Favorite Character Graph. Write in a row on the chalkboard the name of each character in the story. Have each student vote by writing his or her name under the appropriate character heading to form a graph. Analyze the results with the class by having students compare the character with the most votes to the character with the fewest votes. Before removing the graph, have students stand next to the graph, and have one student hold up a copy of the book. Photograph the scene, and add the picture to a reading scrapbook.

Favorite Character Election Ballot

_____'s Ballot

☑ I vote for _____

from the story _____

because _____.

Draw a picture of your favorite character.

Prove It

Purpose

This activity is designed to have students demonstrate an understanding of character traits by rereading to find story support for a selected trait.

Directions

 Copy a class set of the Prove It reproducible.

 Choose a story to read to the class or for students to read independently.

 After reading the story, have students discuss the characters in the story. Brainstorm with the class words that describe each character (e.g., words that tell how each character looks, feels, or acts). Record student responses on the chalkboard or a piece of chart paper.

 Give each student a reproducible. Ask students to select an important character from the story and write the character's name or draw the character's picture in the book at the top of the reproducible.

 Have them write two words that describe their character.

6 Invite students to reread the story to find examples that illustrate the traits they selected.

7 Have them write or draw the parts of the story that illustrate the two traits.

8 Encourage students to discuss their character trait analysis with a partner.

Extension

Give students another copy of the reproducible. Invite them to work with a partner or small group to read other familiar books. Ask students to select important characters, list descriptive words about the characters, and find support in the story for their character descriptions.

Prove It

Choose an important character to draw or write about.

Title _____

Author _____

Important Character

List words that describe the character.	List examples from the story.
1. _____	
2. _____	

Puzzlers

Purpose

This activity is designed to have students record a story's characters, setting, and plot and make comparisons with other characters.

Directions

1. Copy a class set of the Puzzlers reproducible. Gather a class set of envelopes.

2. Have students select a book to read.

3. After students read their story, ask questions to have them brainstorm the story elements. For example, *Who was in the story?* (main characters) *Where and when did the story take place?* (setting) *What happened?* (plot) Record student responses on the chalkboard or a piece of chart paper.

4. Give each student a reproducible. Have students draw and/or write about the main character in the story, where it took place, and what happened.

5. Ask them to cut apart their puzzle, write their name on the back of each puzzle piece, mix up the pieces, and put them back together again to retell the story.

6. Divide the class into pairs, and invite partners to compare their stories to identify similarities and differences in character, setting, and plot.

7. Have students store their puzzle pieces in an envelope. Tell them to write their name and the book title on the envelope.

Extension

Divide the class into small groups. Have group members play a game of Mix-and-Match Storytime by mixing and matching their pieces to create new puzzles. Have students use their mixed-up puzzles to create a new silly story. Invite older students to write out their mixed-up story with additional details and action.

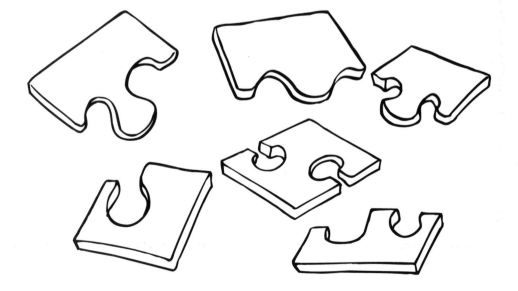

Puzzlers

Complete each part to tell about your story. Cut out each piece.
Mix up the pieces and then put them back together again.

Who?

Where? When?

What happened?

Speak Up

Purpose

This activity is designed to help students understand the differences between narration and dialogue. This activity develops story comprehension and can be used to introduce the literary element of conflict between characters or between the character and his or her conscience.

Directions

1 Copy a set of the Speak Up reproducible. Cut the reproducible in half on the dotted line.

2 Choose a story with many examples of dialogue to read to the class or for students to read independently.

3 After reading the story, have students reread it, using expression to read all dialogue.

4 Discuss the characters in the story and their roles.

5 Give each student a reproducible. Have students select a character and write one sentence of the character's dialogue from the story.

6 Reread or retell the story, and ask students to hold up their speech bubble at the appropriate place in the story and read their sentence.

Extension

Have students use the directions in Story Character Pops (page 46) to create a puppet for their character. Have students work in pairs. Ask one student to hold up the character puppet while the other student reads with expression from the corresponding speech bubble. Have students reread the rest of the book or chapter in this way.

Mr. Pig, Mr. Pig, are you in?

Name _____ Date _____

Speak Up

Character _____

- -

Name _____ Date _____

Speak Up

Character _____

Responding to Literature • 1–3 © 2002 Creative Teaching Press

Story "Mask-querade"

Purpose

This activity is designed to develop story comprehension as well as character analysis and understanding.

Directions

 Make a copy of the Character Mask reproducible. Select the person or animal mask depending on the type of characters in the story the class will read. Cut the reproducible in half, and enlarge it. Make a class set of the revised reproducible. Gather construction paper, feathers, and art supplies.

 Choose a story to read to the class or for students to read independently.

 After reading the story several times, ask the class to select a character to dramatize during another rereading or retelling of the story.

 Discuss the character's features, actions, and possible vocal style (e.g., shrill, soft, animal sound).

Have each student choose a character from the story. Give each student a copy of the appropriate mask pattern and art supplies. Have students cut out their pattern and then use art supplies to create a mask for their character.

 Staple a piece of yarn to each mask.

Reread or retell the story, and invite students to wear their mask and dramatize their selected character's parts.

Extension

Have students work in small groups to create a mask for each character from the story. Encourage students to practice rereading or retelling the story, and then have them use their character masks to perform the story for another class or for parents.

Character Mask

Cut out the person mask. Decorate it to look like your character.

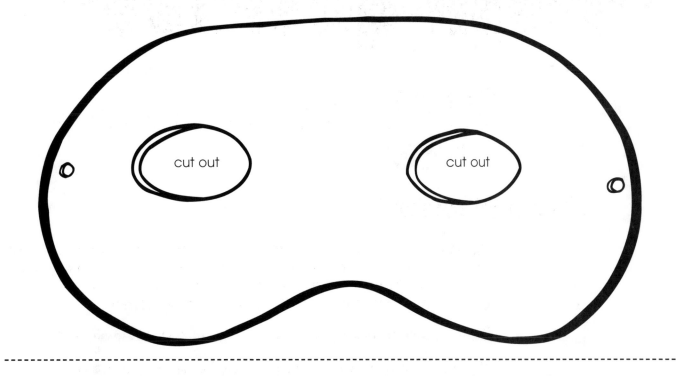

cut out

cut out

Character Mask

Cut out the animal mask. Decorate it to look like your character.

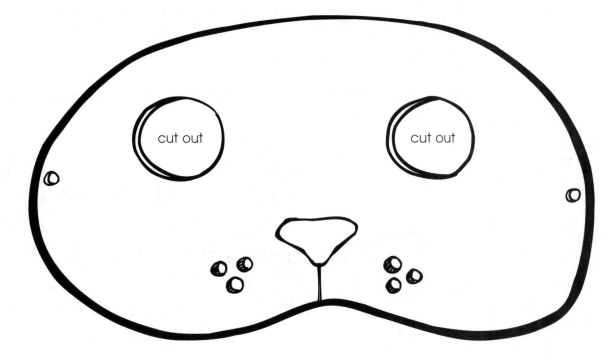

cut out

cut out

Book Beat

Purpose

This activity is designed to help students create stimulating book reports and recall important story details.

Directions

1 Copy a class set of the Book Beat reproducible.

2 Choose a book for students to read twice independently.

3 Give each student a reproducible. Invite students to answer the questions.

4 End the activity by playing music and inviting students to orally present their book reports.

Extension
Tape-record or videotape students during their "book commercials," and place the written reports with the recordings for students to listen to or view during literacy center time and to present to parents during parent conferences or parent night.

Book Beat
Read All about It!

As reported by _____

Answer the following questions about the story.

Where does the story take place?
List the characters in the story.
How does the story begin?
What problem develops in the story?
What is the solution to the problem?
List special words or phrases used in the story and their meaning.

Chill Out with a Story!

Purpose

This activity is designed to help students recognize critical story elements and build story comprehension.

Directions

1 Copy a class set of the Cool Cone Scoops reproducible. Cut out a class set of "ice-cream cones" from brown construction paper. Gather a class set of colored construction paper.

2 Choose a book to read to the class or for students to read independently.

3 After reading the story, brainstorm with the class various parts of the story, such as the title and author. Ask students to think about who the characters are, where the story takes place, what happened to cause a problem in the story, and how the problem was resolved. Record student responses on the chalkboard or a piece of chart paper.

4 Give each student a reproducible, a paper cone, and a piece of construction paper.

5 Have students complete the reproducible independently or as a class.

6 Have them write the book title and author on their cone and then glue it to the bottom of their construction paper.

7 Tell students to cut out the four ice-cream scoops and glue them above the ice-cream cone.

8 Invite students to retell the story to a partner.

Extension

Have students "chill out" with a "cool cone" book report! Place additional copies of the reproducible in a literacy center. Encourage students to independently write their book reports and then present them to the class.

Cool Cone Scoops

Complete the information. Cut out the ice-cream scoops.

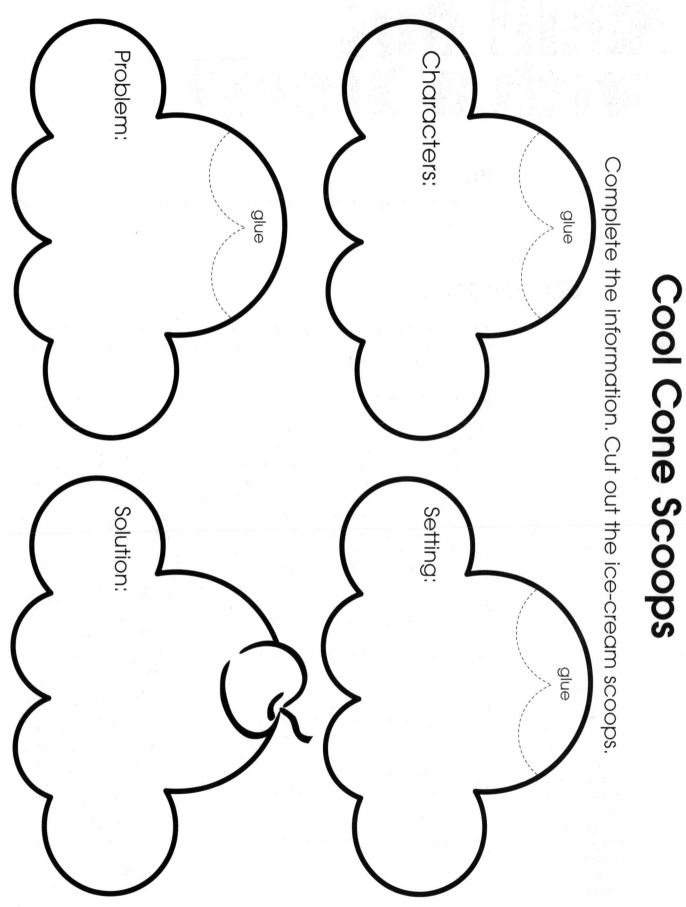

Characters:

glue

Problem:

glue

Setting:

glue

Solution:

Chop, Block, and Read

Purpose

This activity is designed to help students recognize critical story elements. This activity also builds story and content vocabulary.

Directions

1 Copy a class set of the Story Cube reproducible onto tagboard or construction paper. (As an option, enlarge the reproducible to 11" x 17" [28 cm x 43 cm], and copy a class set of the revised reproducible.)

2 Choose a book to read to the class or for students to read independently.

3 After reading the story, brainstorm with the class different story elements (e.g., main characters, setting, their favorite part of the story). Record student responses on the chalkboard or a piece of chart paper.

4 Ask students to look back through the book to recall any new content words or new vocabulary words.

5 Give each student a reproducible. Have students answer the questions *Who? What? Where?* and *When?* and list any new words in the appropriate place on their cube.

6 Have them cut out their story cube and follow the instructions to assemble it.

Extension

Have students present their story cube to the class during a show-and-tell. Encourage them to carefully manipulate the cube as they tell about each part of the story. Use all the new content students wrote on the cubes to create a class word bank.

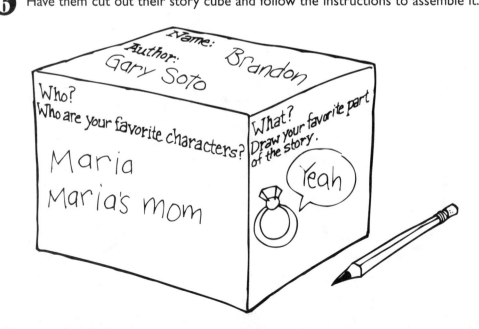

Story Cube

Write or draw pictures about the story. Cut, fold, and glue as indicated.

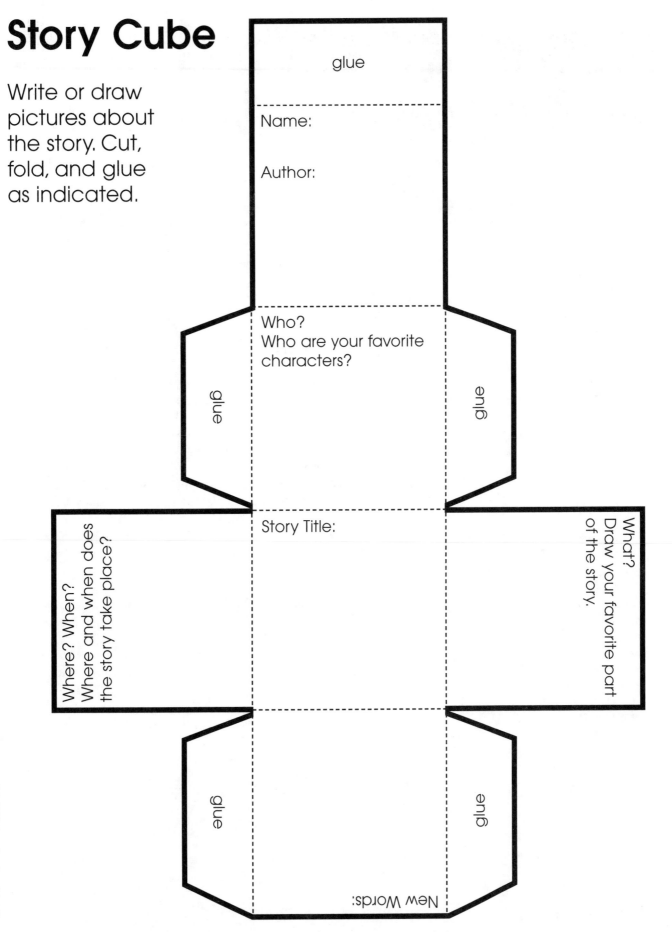

glue

Name:

Author:

glue

Who?
Who are your favorite characters?

glue

Where? When?
Where and when does the story take place?

Story Title:

What?
Draw your favorite part of the story.

glue

New Words:

glue

Draw and Tell Story Journal

Purpose

This activity is designed to have less fluent writers discuss their drawings, share their story, or respond to critical story elements through "story talk."

Directions

1 Copy a class set of the Draw and Tell Story Journal reproducible.

2 Staple several pieces of drawing and writing paper behind the reproducible and staple a piece of construction paper to the back to make a journal for each student.

3 Give each student a journal. Have students color the cover.

4 Have students discuss a story they just read or heard read to them. Ask them to think about one of the following story elements: the important characters in the story, where the story takes place, what happens in the story, how the story ends, what the story makes them think about, or how something a character does is similar to something they do. Record student responses on the chalkboard or a piece of chart paper.

5 Have students open their journal to the first page and respond through drawing and writing to the specific story element the class discussed in Step 4.

6 Give them time to talk about their literature responses with a partner, or give ample time for a number of students to talk about their responses each day until all have had a turn to share.

7 Have students repeat this activity several times throughout the year.

Extension

Obtain an inexpensive blank cassette tape for each student. Each time students share a response from their journal, tape-record their story talk. Have more fluent students also label or write about their drawings. Throughout the year, have students and parents reflect on students' progress in both their drawing in response to literature as well as their story talk. (This journal also makes an exceptional assessment tool to add to each student's individual assessment portfolio.)

Draw and Tell Story Journal

by _____

Give Me 5!

Purpose

This activity is designed to provide young students with an opportunity to recall character traits, recall and write about nonfiction in a paragraph format, and retell a story.

Directions

 Copy a class set of the Give Me 5! reproducible. Prepare a sample reproducible by cutting out the hand and gluing it to a paint-stirring stick.

 Choose a book to read to the class or for students to read independently.

 After reading the story, have students think about the sequence of events in the story.

 Encourage students to talk about how the story started, how the story ended, and three significant events in the story between the beginning and the ending. Record student responses on the chalkboard or a piece of chart paper. As students retell each event, hold up the sample reproducible and point to the corresponding finger.

5 Give each student a reproducible. Have students list the events of the story and cut out their completed hand.

Extension
Staple the completed "hands" on a bulletin board titled *Hands Up for Good Reading*.

Give Me 5!

Write the title, the beginning, three significant events, and the ending of your story.

First Event

Second Event

Third Event

Beginning

Ending

_____
Title

_____
Name

Going on a Story Hunt

Purpose

This activity is designed to help students identify the main characters and plot of a story. Use story maps to assess whether or not students can identify the main actions in the plot that move the story toward its resolution.

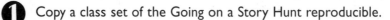

Directions

Extension

Select a different familiar book to use for a "live story hunt." Write *Beginning, Middle,* and *End* on three separate pieces of construction paper. Place the papers on the floor. In between each piece of paper, create a "road" for students to follow. Select one student to tell about the beginning of the story, one student to tell about the middle, and one student to tell about the end. Have volunteers go on the story hunt as other students participate in the knee slap and chant rhythm, pausing at each part of the story for the student assigned to that part of the story to tell about what happened. Have the class continue the rhythm softly as students tell their part of the story.

1 Copy a class set of the Going on a Story Hunt reproducible.

2 Read a familiar story to the class, and then discuss it with them. Ask students to think about each part of the story (beginning, middle, and end) and details from those parts.

3 Lead students in a "story hunt" using the following chant to the rhythm from "Going on a Bear Hunt" and alternating knee slaps. Have students echo each line.

> *Going on a story hunt.*
> *Think very carefully.*
> *What happened first?*
> *What happened next?*
> *How did the story end?*

4 Say *Let's go on a story hunt again, but this time, let's stop to answer each of the questions we asked during the chant.* Repeat the chant, and pause to have students answer the questions. Rephrase their answers rhythmically, so students can repeat the answers as part of the chant.

5 Give each student a reproducible. Have students follow the directions to complete the story map.

Name _____   Date _____

Going on a Story Hunt

Write the title of your story. Draw or write about the beginning, middle, and ending of the story. Draw a picture of the main character.

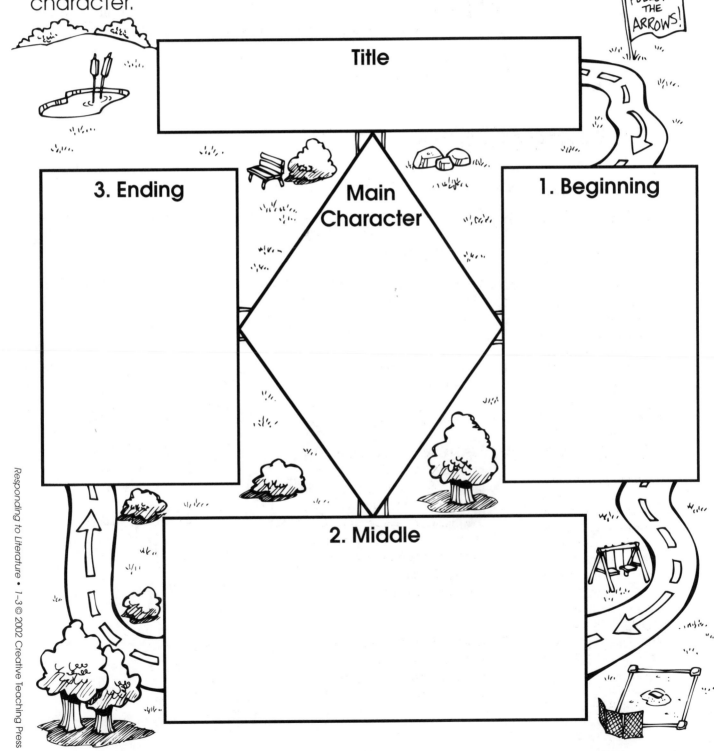

FOLLOW THE ARROWS!

Title

3. Ending

Main Character

1. Beginning

2. Middle

How It Grows

Purpose

This activity is designed to be used after the class reads various nonfiction reading selections about the growth of people, plants, and animals to help students draw and write about those stages.

Directions

 Copy a class set of the How It Grows Story Strip reproducible.

 Read to the class various nonfiction books that describe the growth cycle of plants, animals, and humans.

 Discuss the various growth cycles, and draw on the chalkboard what the stages might look like. For example, draw a baby, a young person, and an adult or a seed, a sprout, and a full grown plant.

④ Ask students to select and think about one of the growth cycles.

⑤ Give each student a reproducible. Ask students to draw on their reproducible the three stages of the growth cycle they selected.

⑥ Have them describe the stages in writing under the story strip.

Extension

Ask students to discuss or write about what a plant, a person, or an animal needs at each stage so that it can continue to grow and prosper. If students are unsure about what is needed, encourage them to conduct research by reading other materials, searching the Internet, asking an older student, or interviewing their parents to gain additional information.

How It Grows Story Strip

Draw a picture of each stage of growth in the boxes. Write a sentence about each stage on the lines.

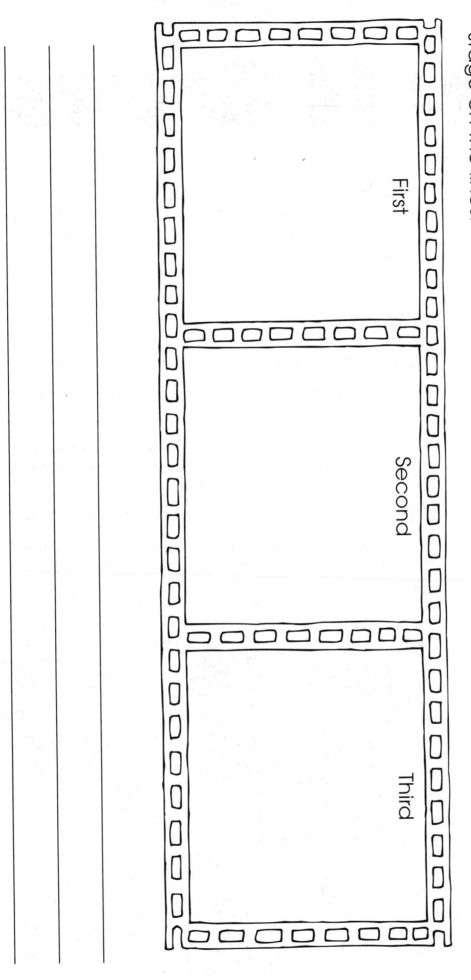

First

Second

Third

Pop Up with a Story!

Purpose

This activity is designed to assist students in writing their own version or retelling of a story.

Directions

1 Copy a class set of the Pop-up Card reproducible.

2 Choose a book to read to the class or for students to read independently.

3 Ask students to discuss the whole story (to determine if they can remember all of it) or summarize all of the important parts of the story. Record their responses on the chalkboard or a piece of chart paper.

4 Give each student a reproducible. Have students cut out the pop-up card, fold as indicated, and then open it up.

5 Tell them to write new vocabulary words or interesting words on the pop-up portion and then draw pictures and/or write (retell) the major events of the story on the card portion.

6 Invite students to share their "story pop-up" with classmates.

Extension
Have students write their name on their "story pop-up." Place the story pop-ups in a literacy center. Encourage students to choose a pop-up, read it, and then "interview" the student who wrote the pop-up about his or her story.

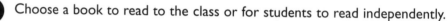

coiled

perched

bristles

tendrils

ambassador

Pop-up Card

Cut out the card. Fold on the dotted lines. Write new vocabulary words or interesting words on the pop-up part and draw pictures or write (retell) the major events of the story on the card part. Fold the pop-up part inside the card.

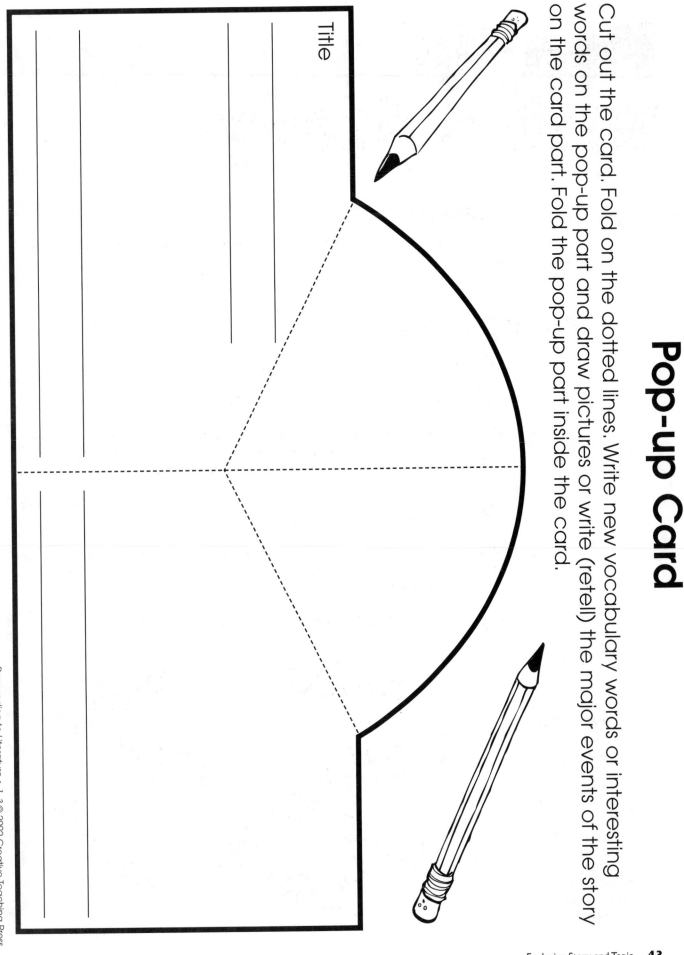

Title

Story Flip Book

Purpose

This activity is designed to help students think about three critical literary elements (the character, the action, and the setting) in an interesting mix-and-match book format.

Directions

1 Copy a class set of the Story Flip Book reproducible.

2 Have each student choose a story to read.

3 After students finish reading their story, brainstorm with the class the main character, one action performed by that character, and where the action took place in various stories. Record student responses on the chalkboard or a piece of chart paper.

4 Give each student a reproducible. Have students answer the questions *Who? What?* and *Where?* about the main character from their story. Ask them to draw a picture of the character according to the directions on the reproducible.

5 Combine all students' pages, cut off the top section, cut on the solid horizontal lines of each reproducible, and bind the pages into a class "story flip book." Place the completed book in a literacy center. Invite students to read the flip book during free time.

Extension

After students finish reading the class-made flip book, have them flip to three different pages and write the text from the Who?, What?, and Where? sections on a piece of writing paper. Encourage them to use this text to write a new nonsense story!

Name _____   Date _____

Story Flip Book

Draw the character's head in section A. Start drawing the neck at the two small dots. Draw the midsection of the body in section B. Start at the small dots and end at the large dots. Draw the rest of the body in section C.

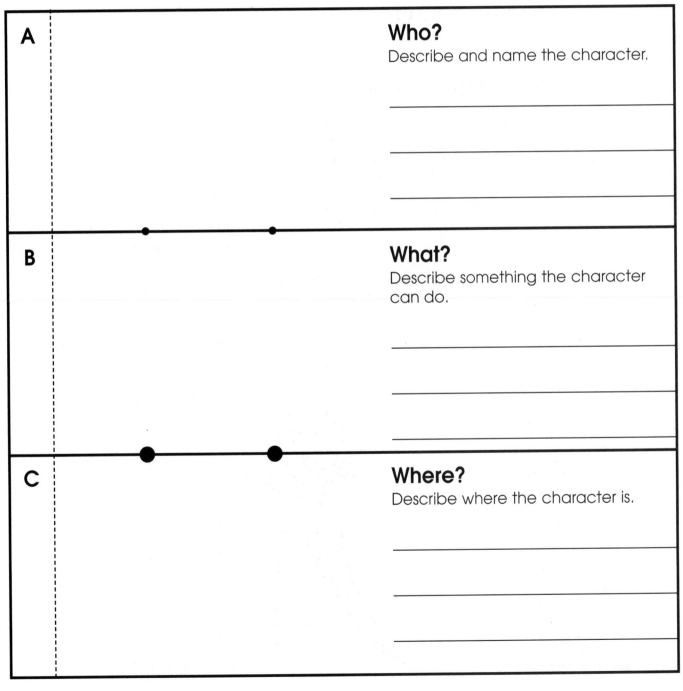

A		**Who?** Describe and name the character.
B		**What?** Describe something the character can do.
C		**Where?** Describe where the character is.

Responding to Literature • 1–3 © 2002 Creative Teaching Press

Story Character Pops

Purpose

This activity is designed to have students create character stick puppets to dramatize their retelling of a story. This activity develops oral language, character analysis, story plot sequence, and story comprehension.

Directions

1. Copy a class set of the Story Character Pops reproducible. Gather craft sticks.

2. Choose a story to read to the class or for students to read independently.

3. After reading the story to the class a few times, ask students to think about all the characters in the story.

4. Have students describe each character's traits and explain his or her significance to the story. Record student responses on the chalkboard or a piece of chart paper.

5. Give each student a reproducible and craft sticks. Invite students to cut out the ovals and create an entire set of "story character pops" for the story.

6. Have them glue their completed story character pops onto craft sticks.

7. Have students place their completed story character pops in a line in the order they appear in the story.

8. Invite them to take turns retelling the story to each other using their story character pops.

Extension

Have students work with a partner or in groups of three. Ask each group to divide one set of character story pops between their group members. Have group members work together to retell the entire story. Ask students to take turns describing the story and dramatizing their characters' dialogue.

As an option, have students use the directions in Speak Up (page 24) to create speech bubbles for each character and use them as they retell the story.

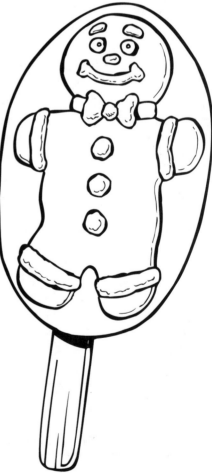

Story Character Pops

Choose four characters from the story. Create each "pop" (oval) to look like a character in the story. Cut out the pops and glue them onto craft sticks.

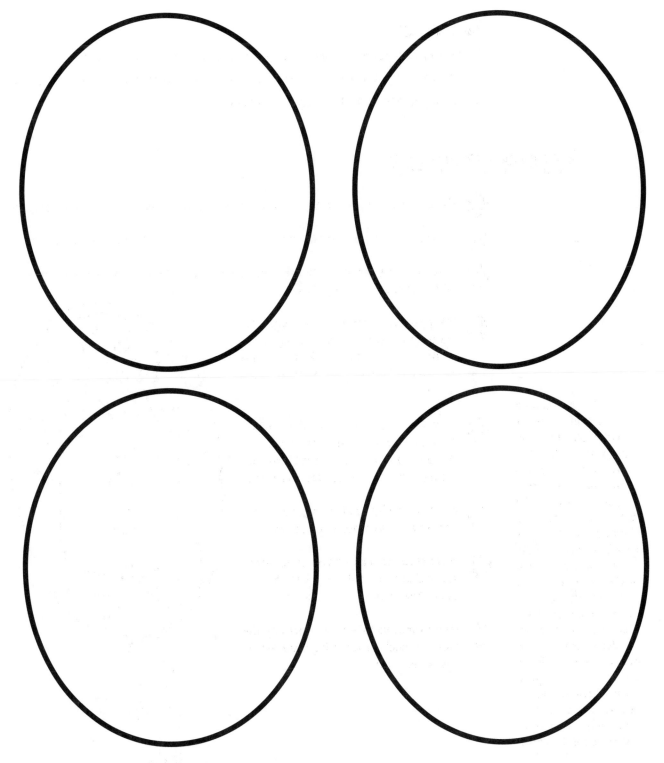

Story Puzzle

Purpose

This activity is designed to have students respond to critical story elements.

Directions

1. Copy a class set of the Story Puzzle reproducible. Gather a class set of envelopes.

2. Choose a book to read to the class or for students to read independently.

3. After reading the story, brainstorm the story elements with the class. For example, have students discuss the main character, the problem, and two actions taken by the characters in response to the problem. Record student responses on the chalkboard or a piece of chart paper.

4. Give each student a reproducible. Have students draw the character's face and list details about each story element in the appropriate section of the reproducible.

5. Tell them to cut apart their "story puzzle," write their name on the back of each piece, and try to put the puzzle back together.

6. Invite students to take turns reconstructing and discussing the story with a partner.

7. Invite them to place their puzzle pieces in an envelope.

8. Place the envelopes in a literacy center, and invite students to put together different puzzles.

Extension

Create a chart-size story puzzle, and cut apart and laminate the pieces. During independent reading or a read-aloud, use black crayon to record details about the story elements on the laminated puzzle pieces to help students think through stories. Reconstruct the puzzle as you write on each piece. Use an old sock to wipe off the writing, and reuse the pieces with new stories.

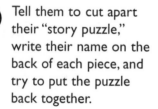

Story Puzzle

Draw the main character's face. List details about the story on each puzzle piece. Cut out the pieces. Find a partner and discuss the story. Put your puzzle back together.

Title:

Other Characters:

Main Character:

Problem:

Action:

Action:

What Is It?

Purpose

This activity is designed to help students recall, write about, and respond to details about nonfiction topics such as animals, plants, or objects.

Directions

1 Copy a class set of the What Is It? reproducible. Gather a class set of small paper bags.

2 Ask each student to select one animal, plant, or object from a current unit of study.

3 Have students brainstorm and write about specific details they learned about their selection.

4 Invite them to work in small groups, with a partner, or independently. Give each student a reproducible and a paper bag.

5 Tell students to use three pertinent details they wrote to create clues and write them on the reproducible.

6 Have them cut out the box on the reproducible and glue it to a paper bag.

7 Give students a piece of drawing paper.

8 Have students draw a picture of the selected item, cut it out, and place it in their bag.

9 Have them read their clues to a partner, invite him or her to identify the mystery item, and then have the partner check the answer by pulling the picture out of the paper bag.

Extension

Have students use the prepared "clue bags" for a game of Super Sleuth—an independent reading, writing, and critical thinking activity. Have students close their bags and display them on a table. Number a sheet of paper (one number for each student), make a class set of copies, and place a paper next to each bag. During the week, ask students to read each set of clues, write on the paper what they think is in the bag, and sign their name. At the end of the week, have students open their bag and reveal their drawing of their mystery item.

What Is It?

Write three clues about the item you selected. Cut out the box and glue it to a paper bag. Shhh! Do not tell anyone about your item. It's a secret!

_____'s Clues

1. _____

_____

_____

2. _____

_____

_____

3. _____

_____

_____

"Sense-ing" the Setting

Purpose

This activity is designed to have students visualize the story setting and think about what they would see, hear, smell, taste, and feel if they were in that setting.

Directions

1 Copy a class set of the "Sense-ing" the Story Setting reproducible.

2 Choose a book to read to the class or for students to read independently.

3 After reading the story, discuss the setting. Encourage students to picture in their mind everything they can think about the setting, including what it would look like, how it would smell, what sounds they might hear, and what they might touch and eat if they were really there. Have students share what they pictured. Record their responses on the chalkboard or a piece of chart paper.

4 Give each student a reproducible. Have students follow the directions to draw the story setting and write about it.

5 Encourage students to share their completed reproducible with a partner.

Extension
Ask students to think about a favorite setting of their own (either from a book or a place they actually have been). Ask them to brainstorm sights, sounds, smells, tastes, and feelings about that special place. Give students another copy of the reproducible, and ask them to write and draw about their own special place.

"Sense-ing" the Story Setting

Where does your story take place (setting)? Draw a picture of the story setting in the box. List what you would see, hear, smell, taste, feel, and know about if you could go there.

The story setting: _____

I see _____.

I hear _____.

I smell _____.

I taste _____.

I feel _____.

I know _____.

Set-the-Stage Story Bag

Purpose

This activity is designed to give students a tool for thinking about and describing the setting of a story.

Directions

 Copy a class set of the Set-the-Stage Story Bag reproducible. Gather a class set of small paper bags.

 Choose a story to read to the class or for students to read independently.

After reading the story, ask students to think about when and where the story took place. Explain that this is called the story's setting.

 Discuss how the setting helps the reader understand the story.

 Ask students *Where do you buy groceries? Where do you purchase gas for your car?* and *Where do you buy clothing?* Explain that the grocery store, gas station, and department store are all examples of settings. Ask *If the setting is a farm, what would it look like?* and *If the setting is a jungle, what would you find there?* Record student responses on the chalkboard or a piece of chart paper.

Give each student a reproducible and a bag. Have students draw a picture of the story's setting on the reproducible, cut out the outline of the bag, and glue it to their paper bag. Encourage students to cut the bag to reflect the setting they drew. For example, if the setting was the beach, students could cut the bag's top to resemble waves. If the setting was a house, they could cut the bag's top to resemble a roof line.

Extension

Ask students to think about what would happen if the story occurred in a different place or time. For example, say *What if the story took place in a rain forest instead of a desert? Would the story be as interesting?* Have the class brainstorm alternate settings for the story and discuss how they would change the story. Have students rewrite or retell the story with a new setting and create a new "story bag."

BOOK TITLE
If You Give a Mouse a Cookie

AUTHOR Laura Numeroff

Set-the-Stage Story Bag

Draw a picture of the story's setting. Cut out the "bag" and glue it to a small paper bag.

Book Title

Author

Gathering Word Gems

Purpose

This activity is designed to encourage students to become familiar with the language used in a story and learn new vocabulary words in a developmentally appropriate manner.

Directions

1 Copy a class set of the Word Gems and Gemstones reproducible onto assorted colors of paper. Gather a class set of small paper bags.

2 Choose a story for students to read.

3 Have students read the story and reread it to identify new words. Give each student a piece of paper. Have students list any new words on the paper.

4 Read aloud a piece of literature that is at a higher level, and pause to think about how the author uses words, simile, metaphor, and descriptive words and discuss any new vocabulary words. At the end of the story, have students discuss the use of the different types of words. Brainstorm new vocabulary words with the class. Record student responses on the chalkboard or a piece of chart paper. Also, list special words or descriptive phrases from the story.

5 Have the class reread all the words on the list.

6 Give each student a reproducible and a paper bag. Invite students to cut out the gemstones from the bottom of the reproducible and cut around the large gem. Have students write their name and book title on the large gem.

7 Have students glue the large gem to their bag.

8 Have students write a word from the class list on each gemstone. Have them write the book title on the back of the gemstones.

9 Give each student a piece of paper. Invite students to create their own gemstones and cut them out. Ask students to write additional vocabulary words and/or descriptive phrases on their gemstones and place them in their "gemstone bag."

10 Have students swap bags and read each other's new words.

Extension

Use a large handled bag to create a class gemstone bag. Invite students to add new gemstones to the bag during literacy center time or during their individual reading experiences. Periodically, choose gemstones from the bag, read the words, and acknowledge the student who contributed each new word.

Word Gems and Gemstones

Cut out the large gem and the gemstones. Glue the large gem to a paper bag. Write vocabulary words on the gemstones and then place them in the bag.

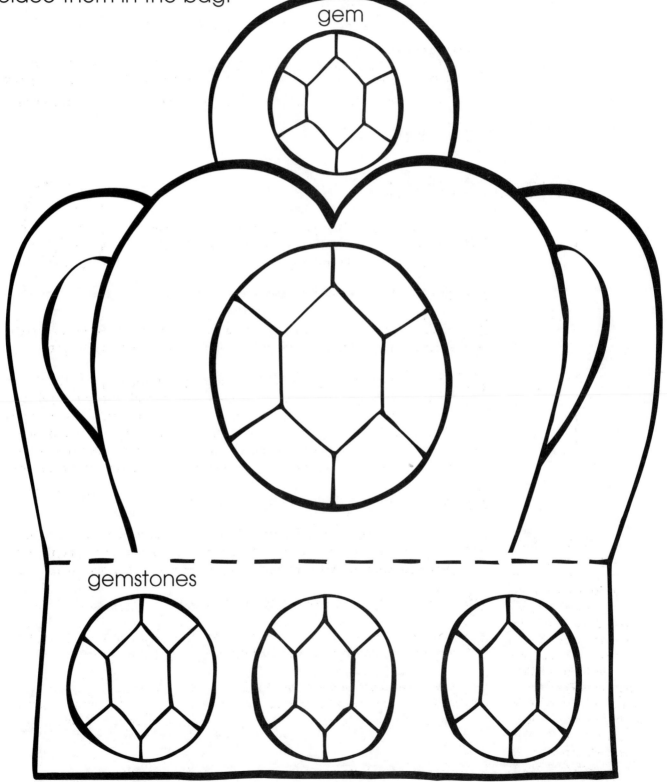

gem

gemstones

Silly Story Song

Purpose

This activity is designed to help students become familiar with syntax, parts of speech, and story vocabulary and think about a story character in association with an action that character performed in the story.

Directions

 1 Copy a class set of the Silly Story Song reproducible.

2 Choose a story that has numerous characters.

3 Read the story to the class. Give each student a piece of paper. Ask students to list all of the characters in the story.

4 Have students write next to each character's name one or two descriptive words and one or two actions performed by that character in the story.

5 Ask students to share their list with a classmate.

6 Select one character, one descriptive word, and one action. Use the format on the reproducible to model how to write a "silly story song" on sentence strips.

 7 Place the sentence strips in a pocket chart, and invite students to sing the silly story song.

 8 Give each student a reproducible. Ask students to use one character, one descriptive word, and one action to create their own silly story song.

 9 Invite students to sing their song to the class.

Extension

Tape-record the class singing each student's song. Place the completed reproducibles and cassette in a listening center, and invite students to listen to the class singing the songs.

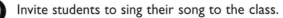

The little red hen baked some bread.
The little red hen baked some bread.
Hi, ho for The Little Red Hen, oh!
The little red hen baked some bread.

Silly Story Song

Complete the blanks with a descriptive word for your character, his or her name, the action word, the action of the character, and the story title. Sing your "silly story song" to the tune of "The Farmer in the Dell."

The _____ _____ _____ _____.
           what kind?   who?   did?   what or where?

The _____ _____ _____ _____.

Hi, ho for _____, oh!
                             Story Title

The _____ _____ _____ _____.

Super Shape-Ups

Purpose

This activity is designed to have students build descriptive vocabulary about main story characters, categorize, and use the newly generated descriptive vocabulary to create a "shape poem."

Directions

 Choose a story that has a cat, dog, pig, or child as a character.

 Cut out the appropriate character from a copy of the Super Shape-Ups reproducible, and enlarge it to full-page size. Copy a class set of the revised reproducible. (As an option, use the revised reproducible to make an overhead transparency to model the directions for the class.)

❸ Read the story to the class, and have students discuss the selected character.

❹ Write *Color and Size, Things It Can Do,* and *Feelings* in a row on the chalkboard or a piece of chart paper. For each category, brainstorm with the class words that describe the character, and record student responses under the appropriate headings. .

❺ Tell students that a poet has to select the most powerful words when writing a poem. Read the words under each heading with the class, and invite students to select the most powerful descriptive word from each category. Place a star next to the selected words.

 Model how to write a "super shape-ups poem" on an enlarged copy of the reproducible. Write the character's name, and below the character's name write the starred words from shortest to longest in length.

Extension

Bind the completed poems into a book. Have two student volunteers decorate a front and back cover. Place the book in a literacy center or class library so students can read and reread classmates' poems. Bind the student-generated word lists for use during future vocabulary studies.

❼ Give each student a reproducible and a piece of writing paper. Have students work independently to generate and write their own descriptive categories on the writing paper and then list appropriate words under each heading. Tell students to select the most powerful word under each heading and use the words to write their own poem on the reproducible. Have students color their poem and write their name on the back of it. (Less fluent students may need to complete this activity in a whole-class setting several times on different days with different characters before they can create their own word lists and poems.)

 Invite students to share their completed poem with the class.

Super Shape-Ups

Vocabulary Tri-Fold

Purpose

This activity is designed to help students build recognition of new vocabulary words and connect word meaning to visual memory.

Directions

1 Copy a class set of the Vocabulary Tri-Fold reproducible.

2 Choose a book to read to students or for students to read independently.

3 After reading the story, have students select one new word they like and hope to use in their own speech or writing.

4 Ask students to picture something in their mind that will help them remember the new word. Explain that this is called a visual memory. Invite students to share their word with the class.

5 Help students think of sentences in which they can use their new word. List the words and sentences on the chalkboard or a piece of chart paper.

6 Give each student a reproducible. Have students write their word from their story, write the word in a sentence, illustrate the sentence, and draw a picture of a memory they have when they think of the word.

7 Have students fold their completed reproducible lengthwise on the solid line and then fold the two vertical sides inward to cover their sentence.

8 Invite students to share their tri-fold with classmates.

Extension

Prepare a large chart paper tri-fold for the whole class to use. Instead of placing each word on a separate tri-fold, have students write their new words in the left column, write a sentence in the middle, and draw a visual memory in the right column. When the chart is filled, create a new one. Use the class-made tri-folds as word banks for student writing.

Nestle

Vocabulary Tri-Fold

My Memory

My Sentence

_____

_____

_____

_____

My Word